AF126402

Northanger Abbey

BY JANE AUSTEN

BOOK ANALYSIS

By Alice Cattley

Northanger Abbey
by Jane Austen

Bright
≡Summaries.com

JANE AUSTEN

ENGLISH NOVELIST

- **Born in Steventon in 1775.**
- **Died in Winchester in 1817.**
- **Notable works:**
  - *Sense and Sensibility* (1811), novel
  - *Pride and Prejudice* (1813), novel
  - *Mansfield Park* (1814), novel

Jane Austen was born in Hampshire in 1775, the daughter of an Anglican rector. Although the Austens had a modest income, Jane and her siblings were encouraged to read widely. She wrote her first spoof novella, *Love and Freindship* (1790) – misspelling deliberate – when she was just 14. Jane apparently read excerpts of the work aloud to her family, developing a writing style characterised by social observation and wit.

In 1801, Jane moved from Hampshire to Bath with her parents and sister Cassandra. Their life in the city was cut short, however, when her father died in 1805. Jane, her mother and Cassandra finally settled in the village of Chawton, where Jane wrote her most famous novels: *Sense and Sensibility*, *Pride and Prejudice*, *Mansfield Park*, *Northanger Abbey* (1818) and *Persuasion* (1818). In 1816, at the age of 41, she became ill and died the following year, possibly of Addison's disease. She continued to write until the very end and is buried in Winchester Cathedral.

NORTHANGER ABBEY

A SATIRICAL GOTHIC NOVEL

- **Genre:** novel
- **Reference edition:** Austen, J. (1974) *Northanger Abbey*. London: Penguin.
- **1ˢᵗ edition:** 1818
- **Themes:** Gothicism, love, imagination, coming-of-age, society

Although *Northanger Abbey* was not published until after Austen's death in 1817, it is widely believed to be her first major work, written as early as 1803. The novel was born out of Austen's disdain for the dramatic and sentimental nature of popular literature, particularly the so-called Gothic novels that were widely read in the late 1700s. *Northanger Abbey* follows 17-year-old Catherine Morland, whose penchant for reading these Gothic novels has given her a dangerously overactive imagination.

As a work of satire, *Northanger Abbey* explores the differences between fiction and reality.

The narrative voice – possibly an incarnation of Austen herself – is frequently ironic, inviting the reader to laugh at Gothic convention. As the story unfolds, we are reminded just how outlandish this convention really is.

SUMMARY

A TRIP TO BATH

17-year-old Catherine Morland, one of ten children, is a girl for whom everyone has modest expectations. While her mother looks after her younger siblings, Catherine spends her days reading novels about girls with prospects far more heroic than her own. She has never been in love, nor even met a suitable man, and mainly experiences the world through fiction. But when the Morland's wealthy neighbours, Mr and Mrs Allen, are prescribed a visit to Bath by Mr Allen's doctor, they invite Catherine to accompany them.

When Catherine and the Allens arrive in Bath, they are struck by the inconvenience of not knowing anyone. With nobody to introduce them and nobody to be introduced to, the first ball they attend at the assembly rooms is a disappointing affair; Mrs Allen spends the majority of the evening lamenting their lack of company while Catherine grows bored. The single perk of the night occurs when Catherine overhears two gentlemen referring to her as "a pretty girl" (p. 46) – a comment which surprises as much as it cheers her. The situation brightens when, at the next ball, the master of the ceremonies unexpectedly introduces them to a gentleman named Henry Tilney. His witty observations leave Catherine keen to see him again – a desire shared by Mrs Allen, who has been most impressed by Henry's knowledge of muslin.

At the Pump-room the next day, Catherine is disappointed not to see Henry. However, she and Mrs Allen are not alone for long; they bump into an old friend of Mrs Allen's, Mrs Thorpe, who is in Bath with her daughters. The eldest, Isabella, soon befriends Catherine. A few days later, Isabella's brother John and Catherine's brother James – who are friends from Oxford – also arrive in Bath. Catherine takes an immediate dislike to John Thorpe, whose rude manners offend her, but as Isabella and James begin to flirt with each other, John appears to follow suit: it is quickly obvious to the reader, though not to Catherine herself, that he intends to win her affections.

A NEW FRIEND

As James and Isabella spend more time together, Catherine finds herself increasingly saddled with John. She seeks alternative company in the form of Henry's sister Eleanor, to whom she is introduced at another ball. Catherine and the Tilneys become good friends and make plans to meet for a walk. On the morning of their arrangement, however, heavy rain seems set to thwart their plan. When the Tilneys are late, Catherine is persuaded by John – who claims to have seen Henry leave Bath that morning – to join him for a ride to Blaize Castle instead. As they speed through the streets, they pass Henry and Eleanor walking towards Catherine's lodgings. Realising that she has been lied to, Catherine begs John to stop. He does not, cementing her dislike for him.

The next day, Catherine rushes to explain herself to Henry and Eleanor. She initially calls at their home, where a servant tells her that nobody is in. When she sees Eleanor and her father General Tilney leave the house shortly afterwards, Catherine believes that she has lost the Tilneys' friendship forever. Bumping into Henry at a play that night, however, things are soon set to rights: Henry explains that his father denied her visit simply because he was about to go out. The pair rearrange their walk and part on good terms.

Yet again, John, James and Isabella attempt to derail Catherine's plans. John even makes excuses to the Tilneys on Catherine's behalf, pretending that she has asked him to convey her apologies. She eventually manages to catch up with Henry and Eleanor and joins them for a walk to Beechen Cliff. They discuss Ann Radcliffe's *The Mysteries of Udolpho* (1794), a famous Gothic novel, and Catherine is delighted to discover that Henry loves reading as much as she does.

The following morning, Catherine learns that Isabella and James have got engaged. James is preparing to go back to Fullerton, where the Morland family lives, to ask his parents for permission to marry. John, who is going to accompany him, leaves Catherine with a series of cryptic remarks about marriage, suggesting that they test the logic of an old song called "Going to one wedding brings on another" (p. 136). Although Catherine's replies are non-committal, John takes them as encouragement, departing with the false impression that she is in love with him.

At yet another ball, Catherine meets Captain Frederick Tilney, Henry and Eleanor's older brother. As James is still in Fullerton, Isabella announces that she has no desire to dance with anyone else – but Catherine and Henry later see her dancing with Frederick. The situation worsens when she receives a letter from James, informing her that his father will give them an income of £400 a year once he is old enough to take it. Although she claims never to think of herself, Isabella is dismayed; it is evident she expected more from Mr Morland.

NORTHANGER ABBEY

Catherine receives a surprise invitation from Eleanor and her father to visit Northanger Abbey, the Tilney home. She is thrilled at the prospect of visiting a real abbey, anticipating hidden rooms and potentially haunted corridors. But before she leaves, she is horrified by the news that John has told Isabella that he plans to propose to her once he returns to Bath. Catherine asks Isabella to write to her brother at once, letting him know that he has been misled. With James still away, she is further concerned by Isabella's continued interest in Frederick.

On the day Catherine is due to depart for Northanger Abbey, she is pleased when General Tilney encourages her to ride in the open carriage with Henry. They spend the journey discussing the Abbey's Gothic potential; Henry is amused at Catherine's imagination and indulges her, describing secret passageways and violent storms. When they arrive, she discovers the Abbey is nothing like the castles she reads about in novels. At dinner that night, General Tilney confuses her by commenting that their dining hall – the largest Catherine has been in – must seem modest compared to those she is used to.

After ransacking a mysterious chest in her room that turns out to contain nothing more exciting than laundry receipts, Catherine allows her imagination to run away with her. Quizzing Eleanor about her mother's death, she becomes convinced that the General had something to do with it. She is suspicious of the fact that he discourages his children from visiting their mother's old rooms and sneaks in to examine them herself. However, she is brought back to reality with a bump when Henry discovers her; realising Catherine's suspicions, he is aghast and chastises her. Catherine, mortified, pledges never to be so fanciful again. Convinced that Henry no longer respects her, she hopes to find comfort in a letter that arrives from James – but the news within it relates the end of his engagement to Isabella, implicating Captain Tilney in the affair.

General Tilney takes Catherine to visit Henry's cottage in Woodston, where Henry is a clergyman. She is exceedingly pleased with it, which in turn pleases the General, who drops several hints about it needing a lady's touch. The next day, Catherine receives another letter, this time from Isabella, who writes that there is nothing between her and Frederick and asks Catherine to let James know that she still loves him. Catherine, finally seeing her friend for what she is, declares to Henry that she wishes she had never met her. Things quieten when the General is called to London and Henry goes back to Woodston for several days.

Then, one night, the General unexpectedly returns. He is furious and tells Eleanor to send

Catherine away from Northanger Abbey the very next morning. Catherine makes the journey to Fullerton alone, convinced that the General has been told of her previous suspicions. She returns home, heartbroken and expecting never to see Henry again. Then, without warning, he arrives at the Morlands' home. He explains to Catherine that John Thorpe misled the General in Bath, claiming that she came from a rich family. Later, after Catherine rejected him, he had bitterly contradicted himself, telling the General instead that Catherine's family was poor. Having hoped to make his son a wealthy match, the General was furious to have wasted time on her and so cast her out of the Abbey. Henry proposes to Catherine, but the couple decide to wait until they can gain the General's consent.

Surprisingly, they are not kept waiting for long. When Eleanor makes a very good marriage, she petitions her father to forgive Henry. In a fit of good humour, he does so, and sanctions Henry's marriage to Catherine.

CHARACTER STUDY

CATHERINE MORLAND

The opening of *Northanger Abbey* leaves the reader in no doubt as to how unremarkable Catherine initially is. Austen informs us that as a child, she is exceedingly plain, with "a thin awkward figure, a sallow skin without colour, dark lank hair, and strong features" (p. 37). She prefers playing cricket to playing with dolls or participating in "the more heroic enjoyments of infancy" (*ibid*.). Indeed, there is nothing heroic about her at all.

Between the ages of 15 and 17, however, Catherine begins to show promise. Her parents observe that she is becoming "almost pretty" (p. 38) and when Mr and Mrs Allen take her with them to Bath, Catherine's life – which hitherto has been as plain as her person – changes forever. Having had a sheltered upbringing with apparently equally sheltered parents (Mrs Morland does not think to warn her daughter against disreputable men, insisting only that she remember to wrap up warm when walking at night), the trip away is her first real experience. As such, *Northanger Abbey* can be considered Catherine's coming-of-age story.

As Catherine is introduced into society, she is perplexed when she starts to receive attention from men; her innocence and lack of experience mean that, while she is accustomed to reading novels, she is terrible at reading people. She repeatedly fails to realise the obvious: she does not notice Isabella's hints that she is in love, is surprised when her engagement to James is finally revealed, and has no idea that John is hinting at marriage before he leaves for Fullerton. Her naiveté simultaneously leaves her unable to pick up on things that are there and, at the other end of the scale, excessively ready to imagine things that are not. It is not until Henry chastises her at Northanger Abbey that she sees the folly of her ways.

HENRY TILNEY

At 25, Henry Tilney is a far more mature and rational character than Catherine. He is less handsome than his older brother Frederick, but still has "a pleasing countenance, a very intelligent and lively eye, and, if not quite handsome, was very near it" (p. 47). He is a clergyman with strong family values, devoted to his sister Eleanor and quick to defend both his father and brother despite their obvious flaws. His determination to win his father's consent before marrying Catherine, even after the General has cast her out of Northanger, is a testament to his enduring sense of filial duty.

In conversation, Henry is light-hearted and eloquent. His propensity to tease Catherine, along with his ironic wit, make his voice strikingly similar to that of Austen's narrator (likely Austen herself). He seems to enjoy playing devil's advocate – somewhat inappropriately for a clergyman – and makes controversial comments in an effort to joke with Eleanor and Catherine:

> "Miss Morland, no one can think more highly of the understanding of women than I do. In my opinion, nature has given them so much, that they never find it necessary to use more than half" (p. 128).

In fact, he is so rarely serious in conversation that his outburst at Catherine upon discovering her in his mother's rooms is all the more shocking. While he has previously encouraged her fancies, now he condemns them – and his words constitute a turning point (a critical moment in which a change takes place) in Catherine's emotional education.

Perhaps it is the baselessness of her assumptions that so alarms him. Henry's rational nature is such that Austen provides her readers with an explanation for his actions, confessing that "a persuasion of her partiality for him had been the only cause of giving her a serious thought" (p. 240). Ever-rational, even in a matter as famously irrational as falling in love, Henry refuses to give his heart where he has no assurance of its being returned – unlike most of the other characters in the novel.

ISABELLA THORPE

Isabella is the prettiest of the Thorpe daughters and knows it. A couple of years older than Catherine, she is apparently worldly-wise and experienced, particularly when it comes to men. She encourages Catherine's interest in Henry Tilney and thrives on having things to discuss:

she begins trivial conversations as though they are highly important, claiming on several occasions to have urgent news only for it to concern the showery weather or a new hat she saw in a shop window.

Prone to exaggeration and deceit, Isabella finally meets her match when she becomes entangled with Frederick Tilney. The harmless flirtation she has enjoyed with men in the past – including going out of her way to ensure that she and Catherine bump into some gentlemen she previously complained were watching her – finally comes back to haunt her like a ghost, appropriately enough for a novel which owes so much to the Gothic.

Although the extent of her relationship with Frederick is never made clear, it is obvious that she expects them to become engaged; a 2007 film adaptation of *Northanger Abbey* shows the couple in bed together, and certainly their relationship is such that the Morlands want nothing more to do with her. If Isabella has had sex with Frederick, she would become a so-called 'fallen woman' – the contemporary name for a woman who indulged in pre-marital sex – and her reputation would be in tatters. Is this no more than she deserves?

ANALYSIS

GOTHIC FICTION

The Gothic genre is defined by its supernatural and sensational elements, such as haunted houses, murder, the macabre, revenge, passion and secrecy. The precursor to modern horror novels, notable Gothic novels during Austen's time included:

- *The Castle of Otranto* by Horace Walpole (1764)
- *The Monk* by Matthew Lewis (1796)
- *The Mysteries of Udolpho* by Ann Radcliffe (1794).

Horace Walpole is generally credited with pioneering the genre of Gothic fiction. He wrote *The Castle of Otranto* to combine elements of medieval romance, which he considered too fanciful, with elements of modern novels, which he thought were too bound to realism. The genre later grew in popularity throughout the 18th and 19th centuries, giving rise to famous works such as *Frankenstein* by Mary Shelley (1818) and *Dracula* by Bram Stoker (1897).

Northanger Abbey was written to satirise Gothic novels, with Catherine serving as a foil to the traditional Gothic heroine. While Gothic heroines are typically 'undone' throughout the course of the novels in which they appear, forced to confront horrors that rid them of their propriety, Catherine herself follows the opposite trajectory. Her journey is one from impressionability to rationality, and the development of her character relies upon the acceptance, as opposed to the rejection, of reality.

The fact that this journey occurs within the setting of an old abbey – a prime location for Gothic horrors – serves to satirise the genre still further. Despite the novel being called *Northanger Abbey*, the majority of the action occurs in the midst of refined Bath society. The name of Northanger Abbey is not even mentioned until at least halfway into the plot; just as Catherine's expectations of the house from its name prove utterly groundless, the expectations a reader might have from the title of the novel prove equally so.

SOCIETY

Horace Walpole contrasted works of romance to works of social realism. *Northanger Abbey* can be classed in the latter category, with many of its characters obsessed with social status and wealth:

- Mrs Allen is described as having "neither beauty, genius, accomplishment, nor manner" but "[d]ress was her passion" (p. 43). With apparently little else to distinguish her, she defines herself entirely by her clothing and invites others to do the same, eager to tell Henry Tilney that her dress cost "9 shillings a yard" (p. 49) and comforting herself with the fact that, even though Mrs Thorpe has children whereas she herself is childless, her dress is obviously more expensive than hers.
- Isabella, in her ambitions to make a wealthy marriage, is what would now be called a gold-digger. Concerned only with social climbing, she pursues Frederick after finding out how little James Morland is worth. When she is left ruined by Frederick, she again tries to win over James, painfully aware that any marriage is better than no marriage.
- General Tilney is concerned with social status over social propriety. His decision to cast Catherine out of Northanger Abbey suggests

that he views her not as a person, but as a commodity; as soon as the reality of her financial situation is made clear to him, he has no concern – or use – for her at all. His favour is eventually 'bought back' by Eleanor, who makes a good enough marriage that the General can 'afford' to let Henry marry Catherine.

THE NARRATIVE VOICE

The omniscient (all-seeing) narrative voice of *Northanger Abbey* is so distinctive that it can almost be considered a character in its own right, offering ironic asides and witty observations throughout the novel. In a book which itself critiques the novel form, the narrator takes on an even greater significance; although Catherine is gently ridiculed for her inability to separate fiction from reality, the narrator – as an incarnation of Austen herself – is guilty of exactly the same thing, presenting the events of the fictional story as though they are facts. This blending of fact and fiction is reinforced by the frequent references to aspects of real life, such as Lord Byron (English poet, 1788-1824), the novels that Catherine reads and the street names of Bath.

Northanger Abbey is ultimately a comedic work and, as such, the narrator can be playful. At the start of the novel, for example, the narrator is so keen to distinguish Catherine from the traditional heroine that she becomes a sort of authorial plaything, characterised by "a thin awkward figure, a sallow skin without colour, dark lank hair, and strong features; - so much for her person; - and not less unpropitious for heroism seemed her mind" (p. 37). The frequent use of dashes in this section serves to make the prose as awkward, inelegant and strongly featured as the girl it describes: a deliberate choice, perhaps, given the narrator's description of novels as being where "the liveliest effusions of wit and humour are conveyed to the world in the best chosen language" (p. 58).

Indeed, the various possibilities of language are explored throughout *Northanger Abbey*. The key events of the plot are all driven forward by words, whether it is John Thorpe's gossip that persuades General Tilney to invite Catherine to Northanger Abbey, Isabella's letter that reveals how duplicitous she really is, or Henry's condemnation of Catherine's overactive imagination that snaps her out of her suspicions.

FURTHER REFLECTION

SOME QUESTIONS TO THINK ABOUT...

- Do you think that the narrator represents Catherine unfairly at the start of the novel? Does this representation change throughout the story?
- In your opinion, is the view of social convention in *Northanger Abbey* ultimately favourable or unfavourable?
- How does Austen play with elements of the Gothic genre?
- How does the character of Henry Tilney compare to other Austen heroes, such as Mr Darcy in *Pride and Prejudice*?
- The novel can be considered a work of social realism. How does this status differentiate *Northanger Abbey* from the fiction mocked within it?
- We know that Austen herself read widely from a young age. Do you think that she is justified in mocking Catherine for her overactive imagination?

- Catherine's parents are worlds away from Captain Tilney. What is the role of parenthood in the novel?
- Do you find Catherine's naiveté endearing or irritating? Why?
- Do you think that Henry is truly in love with Catherine? Consider the reason Austen gives for his proposal and his determination not to marry her without his father's consent.
- Isabella is ruined by a man who has no intentions of marrying her. To what extent is she to blame for her fate?

We want to hear from you!
Leave a comment on your online library
and share your favourite books on social media!

FURTHER READING

REFERENCE EDITION

- Austen, J. (1974) *Northanger Abbey*. London: Penguin

REFERENCE STUDIES

- Milligan, I. (1988) *Studying Jane Austen*. London: Longman.
- Tandon, B. (2003) *Jane Austen and the Morality of Conversation*. London: Anthem Press.

ADAPTATIONS

- *Northanger Abbey* (2007) [Film]. Andrew Davies. Dir. UK: ITV.

MORE FROM BRIGHTSUMMARIES.COM

- Reading guide – *Persuasion* by Jane Austen.
- Reading guide – *Pride and Prejudice* by Jane Austen.

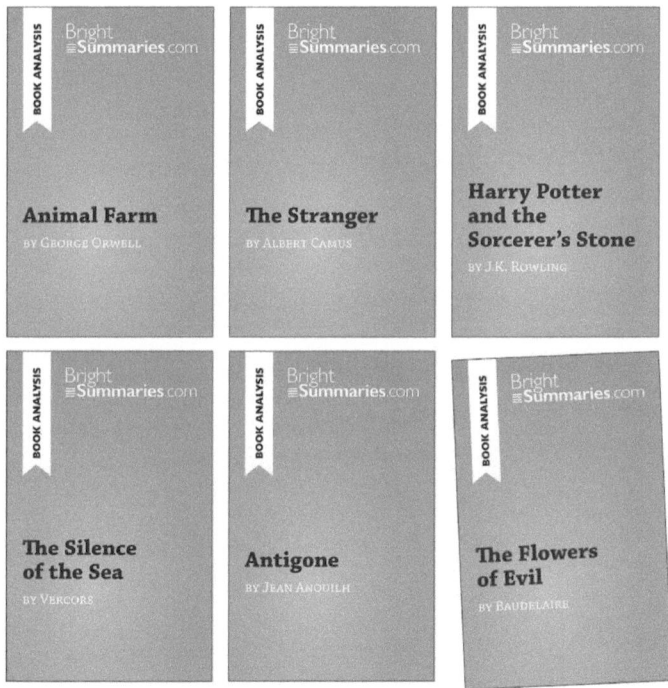

Although the editor makes every effort to verify the accuracy of the information published, BrightSummaries.com accepts no responsibility for the content of this book.

www.brightsummaries.com

Ebook EAN: 9782808012423

Paperback EAN: 9782808012430

Legal Deposit: D/2018/12603/376

Cover: © Primento

Digital conception by Primento, the digital partner of publishers.